Memory Hacks

Memory Hacks

Memory Hacks

15 Simple Practical Hacks to Improve Memory

Life 'n' Hack

ISBN 978-1-544-60893-8

Printed in the United States of America

First Edition

KEYS

INFO UNLOCKED: The Perennial Memory Preservation

- 50 -

.

Memory Hacks

INFO INTRO:

The Perennial Memory Facility

Aging is not for the faint of heart. Perhaps the scariest part of growing older is potentially losing control of your mental faculties. However, contrary to popular opinion, our senses do not have to fade as we age!

There are many things that can be done to preserve your mental health well into your golden years.

Though less common, memory loss can affect younger people as well. The two primary causes of early memory loss are lifestyle and stress. For instance, if you go out every weekend drinking and smoking heavily, you'll risk damaging your brain. The same goes for people with demanding professional lives filled with stress.

Your brain—just like the rest of your body—needs rest to perform at its best and stay at optimum health.

Over time, poor lifestyle choices and stress can gradually lead to the deterioration of memory, both short and long-term. This is why it's critically important to preserve your memory through best mental practices, and the earlier the better.

Here are some major benefits that come with preserving your memory:

- **Productivity**: A more productive life, with the ability to focus and get things done efficiently.

- **Longevity**: Keep your brain active and reduced risk of suffering from memory loss later in life.

- **Adaptability**: The ability to think and react quickly and effectively when necessary in any situation.

- **Capability:** The ability to retain more information in your memory and produce new ideas and solutions.

With that said, we have put together a list of helpful tricks that will help you to improve your memory and keep your mind sharp.

HACK #1:

Bring Memory to Life to the Big Screen

Our first memory hack consists of instantly freezing thoughts, like a recorded playback movie, in order to improve memory.

All you need to do is follow these steps, whenever the need arises:

1. Stop thoughts from flowing into your head by concentrating on a single thought. For example, if you were thinking about salt, visually freeze your focus on salt.

2. Next, bring the thought you are trying memorize to life with an interesting concept, as if you were directing a LARGER THAN LIFE movie scene related to that thought. For example, in your mind's eye see the salt being sprinkled on a dish, or turned into giant crystals, or used as a way to bring the food to life, etc. Why LARGER THAN LIFE? Because things are more unforgettable when they are borderline ridiculous. Think about it—which one would you remember more; someone mundanely sprinkling salt on their fries or someone unconventionally pouring salt on their ice cream?

3. Next, further reinforce that thought with visual mental triggers. Think about any association that came into your mind during step 2, and allow this practice to lead you to trigger new ideas to link back to what you are trying to remember. For example, thinking of salt could lead you to think crystals, salty snacks, beach sand, French fries, etc., and when you think of any of these items, they remind you of salt.

4. Finally, speak everything that comes to mind out loud and concentrate on each thought. You will find your memory is refreshed and your overall thought-process is stimulated. And there you go— congratulations Mr. or Ms. Director on your solid memory movie scene.

ASSIGNMENT: Now, as a first assignment, go through each step. First, freeze your thought into a LARGER THAN LIFE movie scene, and then reinforce it with mental trigger associations. This practice will increase your creativity while also boosting your memory.

HACK #2:

Involve Body Movements to Improve Memorization

We all forget things from time to time. But there's nothing worse than suffering from sudden memory loss when trying to remember how to do something.

The next time you experience memory lapse, try this simple memorization trick by involving body movements:

1. Hold on to a thought and repeat it back to yourself while squeezing your eyes shut and contracting your facial muscles. For example, it could be how to operate a coffee machine that brews a million different fancy drinks and is confusing to use.

2. While holding this position, slightly rock your body from left to right, still holding on to that thought.

3. As you rock and hang on to your thought, start counting: step 1, step 2, step 3, step 4 (or simply count 1, 2, 3, 4). Allow your memory to reveal the different steps, paths to follow, etc. Think of it like memorizing dance moves by numbering each step "And 1 and 2, and 1, 2, 3, 4."

4. Take a deep breath, relax your facial muscles while keeping your eyes closed, and visualize the entire process presented to you.

This time you are not only memorizing what your eyes see, you are involving your body movements into the memorization process. Thus, your body movements can help you re-trigger that sensation to remember how to operate the coffee machine again.

<u>ASSIGNMENT</u>: Now, it's your turn to experiment with this memory boosting trick, by carefully following these guidelines.

HACK #3:

Filter Thoughts through Memorization Isolation

Multi-tasking may be a necessity given our fast-paced lives; however it can easily clutter your mind and ruin your memory if you aren't careful.

The key is to develop discipline over your thoughts to establish a focal equilibrium to balance your thoughts, as this will go a long way in preserving your memory.

One way to accomplish this is through memorization isolation:

1. Open your eyes wide, and take note of all the thoughts in your mind at this very moment. For

example, perhaps you see a cake on a table and a white kitten on the floor, while you are trying to remember how to make a baked omelet and are dreaming of driving the latest Fiat. That is one cluttered mind!

2. Imagine a pie chart divided into equal portions. Place each thought in its own pie "slice."

3. Now enlarge one portion of the pie to emphasize the idea you want your mind to focus on. For instance, trying to remember how to make a baked omelet.

4. Focus on this portion and allow the other thoughts to fade to the back of your mind.

5. Calmly concentrate on this single thought and allow your memory to recreate the details of the issue at hand. For example, a baked omelet requires bacon, salt, eggs, milk, seasoning, chopped tomatoes and cheese. You will cook the bacon in a pan, and then add the eggs, milk, and salt. Add cheese and tomatoes then bake.

6. Once the steps are clear, repeat them in your mind to commit them to memory. You'll discover how quickly the details will come back to you the next time you need them after going thought this memorization isolation episode.

ASSIGNMENT: Try performing memorization isolation and take your time processing each thought, then organize them and filter them by following the guidelines given above.

HACK #4:

Surprisingly Sweet Memory Boost

Eat chocolate. No, really! Eating chocolate is beneficial to the mind and the positive effects are noticeable.

If you don't believe it, just watch a toddler's reaction to eating candy. You will see what people often call a "sugar rush." This rush can benefit you when you need an instant boost to get your memory back on track.

Below you'll find a few guidelines to follow...yes, guidelines to eating chocolate:

1. Choose pure, dark chocolate over any other kind of chocolate (regardless of how much you love your milk chocolate).

2. Quantity is key! Take two squares and allow them to slowly melt in your mouth. Close your eyes, and really savor the taste to make it last.

3. Notice how the sugar and cocoa awaken all your senses.

4. Now open your eyes and focus on what you wish to concentrate on. For example, you want to prepare a dance routine by committing each step to memory so you can execute a flawless performance.

5. Finally, let the taste of the chocolate guide you through the process of registering all the necessary information. You will now be ready to use the information you have stored in your mind.

ASSIGNMENT: Now, let's see if you too can do it on your own. Grab a bar of dark chocolate and use it when necessary, as shown in the guidelines above. See, wasn't that so hard? It's that simple!

HACK #5:

Memory Oxygenation

Proper brain function requires oxygen. Getting the right amount will help you stay alert and maintain your memory throughout the day.

One way to improve or optimize your breathing is to follow these steps:

1. Put your hands flat on a table or any other flat surface.

2. Begin by exhaling slowly, while counting to ten and pushing air out of your lungs until you feel your stomach go completely flat.

3. Inhale slowly, counting to ten, and let the fresh air enter your lungs. Visualize the oxygen making its way into your bloodstream and travelling up to your brain, like water flushed inside your head.

4. Exhale with a big "Ah" sound, mentally counting to ten as you empty your lungs completely. Picture the air refreshing your memory as if they were little bubbles of oxygen exploding in your brain and awakening your deepest thoughts, getting you ready for your next task.

You now have a freshened, invigorated memory.

ASSIGNMENT: It's your turn to try this breathing technique and let it refresh your memory, like oxygen bubbles reaching your brain.

HACK #6:

Mental Mantra Stretching

Just as stretching is key to any total-body workout, your brain needs some "stretching" as well!

Exercising your mind benefits the memory as it helps you relax and process information more effectively throughout the day.

Here's how you should proceed with your mental-stretching session:

1. Stand or sit still.

2. Take a deep breath in. Place your fingers on your temples, breathe out slowly and start making a "hum" sound by stressing the "m" sound for several seconds.

3. Next, let the vibrations emitted by the "m" sound reverberate in your head, like a small massage. This sensation will relax your body and mind and refresh your senses.

4. Repeat the process several times and let the mantra deepen your relaxation while awakening your senses. After a few minutes, you will develop a boost of energy to get you through the rest of your day.

ASSIGNMENT: As practice, try this out anytime during the day when you need a boost. Relax and enjoy the great massaging vibrations that the "hum" sound can bring, as shown in the guidelines above.

HACK #7:

Verbal Memory Anchoring

Certain words or phrases have certain way of triggering the memory simply by saying them out loud. In such a way, they act as the "lucky charm" of your brain. It's not that these words have magical powers but simply as an anchor for pulling information out of your head quickly when you need it.

Here's how to perform such memory anchoring:

1. Find a triggering phrase such as "Booyah!", "Eureka", "Bingo", "I call you", "Come to thee", etc. Try to use a phrase that comes naturally to you.

2. Next, focus on what you wish to accomplish—get more mental energy, preserve your memory, or simply remember something.

3. Count to ten, and then place your fingers on your temples and concentrate for a moment. Drop your head back, look up to the sky and say your triggering phrase aloud several times, as loud as you wish. Flex your facial muscles every time you say your phrase.

4. Let the words open your mind, anchoring what you want to remember into the meaning of that phrase. You'll discover clarity of mind and the ability to easily recall information.

ASSIGNMENT: Now, try memory anchoring for yourself! Remember to let yourself go and pronounce your "magic words" as you anchor it to a thought so that when you say that word again it will trigger your recollection.

HACK #8:

Mindful Memory Recollection

The amazing thing about using visualization methods to simulate memory is that these experiences often feel very real even if they are not, because how does the mind play back actual memory? In visual images. It's almost like playing a video game that immerses you so entirely that you forget all about the passage of time.

Using this same idea, this method will "inflate" your memory like a balloon:

1. Close your eyes and visualize a balloon inflating. Let this balloon represent your memory storage.

2. Take a deep breath and let whatever thought comes to mind to take over. It will seem as if you are looking

directly into the dark depths of your mind. This is the "moment of pause" where you can recover information, redirect a thought, or refresh your memory by being aware of what matters and what doesn't.

- For example, at such moment of pause, you might remember a tricky math equation, or what your friend said the week before, etc. You might find yourself in a state where you can solve problems easier than before.

3. When you start to feel your original intent moving away, visualize the balloon deflating while counting to 5 At this point, instead of seeing the darkness you were seeing in the "moment of pause" you are coming back seeing the light once again.

This may all seem a little new-agey, but the purpose of visualizing the inflating balloon is to act as a symbolic way of helping you calm yourself, practice mindfulness and dig deep into your mind to recollect your thoughts.

ASSIGNMENT: Try doing this yourself and remember to attain this "moment of pause" by visualizing a balloon inflating as a representation of your mind inflating like a balloon.

HACK #9:

Activate Acupressure Points for Better Memory

There's nothing worse than having a killer headache. While facial massage is a well-known technique for easing headaches, you might be surprised to find it can improve your memory as well.

With the help of your fingers, do these steps:

1. Use your index and middle finger to make circular movements by slightly pressing them against the area underneath your ears, moving up to your cheeks, your temples, and then your forehead.

2. Keep doing these same movements, this time working downward from your forehead, to your temples, then your cheeks and underneath your ears.

3. As you massage your face, you will notice the pressure against your skin will feel like electrical charges stimulating your memory. Let yourself relax into this sensation while it engages your nerves and sends energizing vibes to your brain.

4. Repeat the process ten times. You'll feel an overwhelming relaxation take over your upper body (from your shoulders to the top of your head), similar to how you feel after stretching.

ASSIGNMENT: Try it on your own now, and remember to make circular movements with pressure from your fingertips, moving upward then downward (underneath your ears, on your cheeks, temples and the forehead).

HACK #10:

Memory Source Scanning

This is best utilized for problem-solving. It will help you focus your mental energy and develop creative solutions.

Here is how to go about accomplishing this:

1. Calm your body by breathing in and out slowly. You want to be sure your body is relaxed and still to ensure satisfactory results.

2. Start analyzing your thoughts, one after another, allowing yourself to go through each and every detail. For example, suppose you need to make a decision right now about your kitchen renovation being over budget. You will begin recollecting the reasons why you wanted to renovate your kitchen:

- needed new updated appliances and equipments
- wanted to make a fashionable interior statement
- tired of looking at the same old uninspiring floors
- etc.

3. At this point, you are relying on a memory to what led you to set out to make this decision in the first place. As you process the information you can either write down ideas or speak them aloud.

This will help you develop creative solutions to whatever problem you need to solve.

ASSIGNMENT: Now try memory scanning to test if it's effective for you when you need to solve a complex problem that requires to rely on a memory.

HACK #11:

Icy Cold Adrenaline Memory Boost

Adrenaline is a hormone secreted by the body that stimulates the mind and body and spurs it into motion. Though most people think of adrenaline as a part of physical exercise, it can be used to strengthen your brain power as well.

The good news is that you don't need to go to the gym to get an adrenaline rush—you can get it flowing by doing this next application.

Imagine you are outside on a cold day trying to warm your body up:

1. Increase your breathing rhythm to get the right level of excitement. All you have to do is breathe by counting

1, 2, inhale, 1, 2, exhale. Rub your hands together fast while maintaining the same breathing rhythm as in this step. (Repeat this process until you have done 15 inhales and 15 exhales).

2. Next, press your warmed hands on your cheeks and count to 4 and puffing air out.

3. Repeat step 1 and 2 for a total 5 times.

4. As you get more excited, you will feel your heart pumping more blood into to your veins. In turn, this will increase circulation to your brain, giving you a boost of mental energy.

5. Finally, take advantage of this mental state and start exploiting your memory to the fullest, as ideas and information start to emerge.

ASSIGNMENT: Do this yourself and take advantage of he resulting boost of energy. Evaluate how effective your memory works once you stimulated the adrenaline throughout your body and compare it to how productive you are when you are calm.

HACK #12:

Chai Sensory Stimulation

Chai tea, which originated from India, is full of exotic flavors and is a natural source of antioxidants that can enhance the memory. It is typically made by combining traditional black tea leaves with spices like ginger, cinnamon, ground cloves and cardamom. It can be made on your own from scratch or you can buy chai tea packets at the grocery store.

The next time you are in need of some memory stimulation, fire up your tea pot.

1. Pour hot water over the tea leaves and let it step for a minute or two. Remove the bag or strain out the loose leaves.

2. Sip once on the tea, then count to 10 and take two more sips. Pause for ten seconds and let the tea "crawl" into your senses.

3. At each pause, breathe in and out to oxygenate your brain. The key to taking in all the benefits of your tea session is by alternating sipping and breathing.

Once you've emptied your cup, you'll find that you've flushed out the "dust and spiders" from your brain and can make use of your refreshed and dynamic memory.

The thing about remembering things better is that you do want to involve all your senses rather than just what you see or hear but combine all that with what you feel.

ASSIGNMENT: Now it's your turn to take advantage of the memory-boosting powers of chai tea. Heat yourself up a delicious cup and enjoy!

HACK #13:

Simple Shape and Symbol Substitution

The amazing thing about mental imagery is that it helps you personalize the memory process. Shapes and figures are always easy to remember, which makes them an effective tool to involve to help with memorization.

Here's how you can use shapes or figures:

1. Let's say that you are trying to remember to water the boss's plants, correct the typos on your report, make a doctor's appointment for your stepmom and go buy coffee for Tom.

2. Think of a shape, symbol, or figure to represent these things. Pick something familiar, meaning things you see every day. This will make the process even easier

41

and faster than jolting them down everything as texts on paper.

<u>Example</u>:
water the boss's plant = a normal green plant
correct typos on report = a plain sheet of white paper
make doctor's appointment = a guy in a white lab coat
go buy coffee = a typical coffee mug

You may even draw these things out if you want, instead of writing them out as words. This is especially great if you want to be cryptic and not let anybody know what you are doing.

3. Next, visualize each shape slowly scrolling down your eye's mind. Make sure you keep your eyes wide open (try not to blink) through the whole process.

4. Repeat this visualization process one more time. After you are done seeing your list of information, move your eyes around the edge of each shape. For

instance, if it's a circular-shape item, circle your eyes around it with slow eye rotations.

5. When done, blink twice, to "step out" of the session. You are now ready to use the chosen shape or figure as a memory tool.

ASSIGNMENT: Try this yourself. Take your time shaping, symbolizing, or forming things into what they look like and committing the information to memory.

HACK #14:

Grouping with Personalized Clues

When it comes to memorization, it is far easier to remember things when they are broken up into categories or groups.

For example, why do you think we add "-" between our phone numbers and social security numbers? It is because "18006372965" seems more overwhelming for the mind to commit to memory than broken up "1-800-637-2965".

With that in mind, we are going to take this a step further by setting up personalized grouping.

Remember Hansel and Gretel leaving a trial of pebbles behind to ensure they won't get lost? In this fun memory workout, you will use these groups to act as a trail of pebbles in your own mental forest.

Here's one possible personalization:

1. Think of all the things you want to remember. For example, it could be a lesson you've just learned, a grocery list, or a small speech, etc.

2. Divide the information into 5 sections and place a dot between each section. So, if you are making a grocery list, divide your list in five by marking a dot at the end of the 5 segments using physical items. For example, dot 1 broccoli, dot 2 fish, dot 3 dishwashing liquid, etc.

3. Start memorizing your list by visualizing the dot that comes after the last word of a segment. These dots serve as your "tail of pebbles" in your mind.

4. Finally speak out loud the marked words (the ones ending each segment) and let the details comprised in that segment to reveal itself in front of your eyes. To make things more effective repeat this last step if necessary.

The point of all this is, always break large quantities of things to remember into manageable groups. Your brain will love you for it!

ASSIGNMENT: Try grouping things with clues when you need to memorize long lists or complex content.

HACK #15:

Linear List Linking (LLL) Sequence Story

Have you ever had to remember a long series of lists? How about never having to jolt them down again? Well, now you can if you master this technique of linking all the items in the list together as a linear story.

Here is how this powerful technique works:

1. List all the items/information you have to remember.

Example:

Today I must...

- cook pasta with special sauce

- workout
- write dictation for my son
- update a job description
- buy some flour

2. Now link them all together in chronological sequence with a memorable but ridiculous story.

- For example, visualize yourself cooking pasta with a special sauce made from tomatoes an alien gave you. As you are stirring the pasta, the pasta tells you to go help your son with his dictation. While helping your son with his dictation, your bossy son demands you update your job description or he will hate you for the rest of his life. So, you update your job description and miraculously it generates interest from an employer who is a living, breathing flour package.

3. Replay your entire story one more time.

oila! You have now simplified your list of information
into one unforgettable crazy story. It may take some
ractice, but it's really not that difficult. All it takes is a
ttle creativity and imagination.

SSIGNMENT: Now, it's your turn to attempt this linear
st linking. Remember to complete each step of the
echnique by taking your time to get as wildly creative and
diculous as possible because remember...ridiculousness is
ie key to being unforgettable.

INFO UNLOCKED:

The Perennial Memory Preservation

There is nothing more precious than our memory. It holds our treasured childhood experiences as well as crucial information we rely on each and every day.

The greatest athletes, actors, authors and leaders of our times have become who they are as a result of past experiences they hold in their memories. The remarkable genius and incredible talent exhibited by the people we admire most is the direct result of a highly-functioning, well-maintained memory.

Though most of us find our memory failing us a bit from time to time, it's important to recognize that the path to mental agility is not found through a magic pill. Just like physical fitness, mental fitness is best achieved through exercise.

Memory enhancement is simply applying easy-to-follow steps in reshaping how you process what you store in your memory, like the ones we've presented—eating chocolate or drinking chai tea while learning something new, practicing mental visualization, utilizing breathing techniques or creating an adrenaline rush.

You will be able to take possession of your mind and everything in it.

In conclusion, now that you understand how easy it can be to sharpen your memory, what are you waiting for? Be unforgetful by being unforgettable in your new way of memorizing anything.

.

Printed in Great Britain
by Amazon

44341083R00030